Lord

I AM COMING

RACHEL LUGO

Lord
I AM COMING

Reflections on Responding to God's Call

Lord I Am Coming
Reflections on Responding to God's Call
by Rachel Lugo

DEDICATION

To Kendall and LaVonne Patrick. They introduced me to their First Love and have continually shared their excitement and joy from walking with Him. Their devotion to Jesus has been a light in my life and a beacon during my own dark days. Having them for parents has been a gift every day of my life.

To my outstanding husband, Daniel Desi Lugo. You have supported me, encouraged me, and been so very kind throughout this writing process. Thank you for believing not only in word, but also in deed, and for seeing the best in me.

TABLE OF CONTENTS

FOREWORD

IN THE EARLIEST PORTION of the human story we find the introduction of a concept that we humans have struggled with ever since sin broke our world—stopping. We were designed for eternity, but sin brought us death. We were designed for a garden that provided for our needs, but sin brought us pain and sweat and scarcity of provision. The results are that we are perpetually under the pressure of a lack of time and a lack of provision. Into this world steps our Savior and calls to us, "Stop." Stop and believe me for eternity. Stop and believe me for my provision. Stop and come talk with me.

Rachel Lugo has written this devotional out of her desire to stop and talk with her Savior. In it you will find scriptures, thoughts, questions, prayers, and directions regarding praise and thanksgiving. All of these will help you to stop and talk with your Savior.

I encourage you to use this book as an opportunity, even an excuse, to stop for a few moments each day. If the busyness of a particular day impedes your stopping, reject the condemnation that we are so prone to imposing on ourselves. Instead, simply stop and steal away a few moments to return to talking with your Savior with this devotional as a guide. Trust your Savior that he holds eternity and provision in his hands, and he can multiply the time and effort you spend with him back into your life.

I highly recommend this book and I encourage you to stop and use it. It will bless your days!

Dr. Steven J. Beardsley
Senior Pastor, Newark United Pentecostal Church

INTRODUCTION

My heart has heard you say, "Come and talk with me." And my heart responds, "LORD, I am coming" (Psalm 27:8).

I COME TO GOD DAILY. I come with dreams, wants, needs, emergencies, and a desire to please Him. I come in obedience to His Word. Over all the noise of the day, I hear Him call to me, asking me to join Him. These words resonate within me as the pace of life continually threatens to distract me from His voice:

> I know all the things you do. I have seen your hard work and your patient endurance. I know you don't tolerate evil people. You have examined the claims of those who say they are apostles but are not. You have discovered they are liars. You have patiently suffered for me without quitting. But I have this complaint against you. You don't love me or each other as you did at first! (Revelation 2:2–4)

But I am doing this for my first love, my mind screams. *Jesus is my foundation, the center of my decisions, and the One to whom I have committed my life.*

Again, He calls, and the Scripture washes over me:

> As Jesus and the disciples continued on their way to Jerusalem, they came to a certain village where a woman named Martha welcomed him into her home. Her sister, Mary, sat at the Lord's feet, listening to what he taught. But Martha was distracted by the big dinner she was

3

preparing. She came to Jesus and said, "Lord, doesn't it seem unfair to you that my sister just sits here while I do all the work? Tell her to come and help me." But the Lord said to her, "My dear Martha, you are worried and upset over all these details! There is only one thing worth being concerned about. Mary has discovered it, and it will not be taken away from her" (Luke 10:38–42).

At these words, the business of my day begins to fade, the importance of my to do list diminishes, and my heart cries out to my Redeemer, "I am coming!"

This book is a response to the call of our Savior, the One our heart longs for. My hope is that you find yourself sitting with the One your soul desires, putting yourself in His arms, and truly returning to your first and only love, Jesus Christ.

SILENCED:
LIVING LIFE IN A CHOKEHOLD

IN YOUR BIBLE

Mark 4:3–8, 14–20

FOCUS VERSES

Other seed fell among thorns that grew up and choked out the tender plants so they produced no grain (Mark 4:7).

The seed that fell among the thorns represents others who hear God's word, but all too quickly the message is crowded out by the worries of this life, the lure of wealth, and the desire for other things, so no fruit is produced (Mark 4:18–19).

AS WE RESPOND to the call of Jesus, we look toward Him and are amazed at the "foliage" we look through. It seems the more we push towards Him, the more obstacles we find in our path. This overgrowth silences our voices. We realize we are separated from our Savior.

We have not walked away from Him, nor do we desire another, but we find ourselves like the plant in Mark 4:18–19. This plant was not stolen, nor did it fall away. There was simply no room in its surroundings to bear fruit. It was choked, and we are too!

It is impossible to separate the physical and spiritual, for both make up who we are. We are affected, not in part, but as a whole. The plant in the Focus Verses was healthy and growing, evidenced by the fact that thorns had to grow up to choke it. We may be growing, maturing, and looking healthy, but perhaps some of the symptoms listed previously are beginning to creep in. Is it possible that we are choking on life?

Jesus said the plant was crowded (choked) out by the "worries of this life, the lure of wealth, and the desire for other things." As we look at the following list, do any of these symptoms apply to you?

☐ Do I allow the busyness of life to distract me?

☐ Do I have headaches or chest pains due to stress?

☐ Do I look or feel miserable as I rush through my day?

☐ Do I have trouble thinking clearly?

☐ Do I feel exhausted?

☐ Do I feel out of spiritual energy?

☐ Do I take time to meditate on Scripture and spend time with God?

The marked boxes in this list are not marks of condemnation, but rather marks of humanity. No one is alone in wrestling with these symptoms. There are days when we struggle and must ask ourselves, "Am I living life in a chokehold?"

This question demands a response. If something was choking you, wouldn't you do everything in your power to remove the object? Should we not do the same when it is our spirit that is choking? Is it possible that other voices, demanding to be heard, are influencing your schedule, determining your priorities, and slowly pushing your spirit's cry for help further and further down the list until your spirit is silenced?

FOCUS THOUGHT

Am I being choked by life?

A single prayer, self-help book, worship service, or sermon will not remove the things that are choking us. It will only bring a temporary relief at best. Only consistent time with the One our hearts desire will clear away the debris, restore relationship, and allow the growth of fruit as we respond to Jesus' call.

Through these devotions we will begin to remove things that may have crowded in. We will receive nourishment from the soil (through the Word of God), spiritual oxygen (through prayer), a rejuvenating wind (through praise), the warmth of sunlight (through thanksgiving), and specialized fertilizer (through requests) so we will have room to grow and respond to our first love Jesus Christ.

PRAYER

Lord Jesus, I hear you calling me to You and I am responding, "Here I am, I am coming." As I look to You, I find things that have grown up around me, blocking me and trying to choke out our relationship. Please help me to identify the thorns and weeds and pull them out. Give me the strength and courage to face the truth, faith to know that You are with me, and the joy that comes from knowing You are waiting for me.

PRAISE

Read aloud Psalm 118:21–29

THANKSGIVING

Write out why you are thankful that God is calling you.

_____

_____

_____

_____

_____

_____

_____

ASK WITH BELIEF

As you studied through this chapter, no doubt things came to your mind that are blocking you from God's call. List them here. You must be honest with Him, just as David was in the Psalms.

_____

_____

_____

_____

_____

_____

_____

_____

2

BUSYNESS:
A HARSH MASTER WHO
DOESN'T PAY WELL

IN YOUR BIBLE

Job 1; Luke 10:38–42

FOCUS VERSE

There is only one thing worth being concerned about. Mary has discovered it, and it will not be taken away from her (Luke 10:42).

ONE OF THE PROMINENT THINGS choking our society is the trap of busyness. The list of things to get done seems endless. Needs press in on us, and the voices vying for our attention are deafening. How did we get so busy, and do we have to live this way to get things accomplished?

When asked to think of someone (in the Bible) who was busy, perhaps Martha comes to mind. Poor Martha always gets a bad rap, but someone must get the work done, right? What did she do wrong? What could she have done differently? Was it possible for her to have a full schedule and not be busy? What does "busy" even look like, for that matter? For this study, busy is when our attention is consumed by something to the unintended exclusion of others, or a frenzied pace in which we feel trapped.

Martha may have been getting oodles accomplished, but she bought into the busy mindset. The busy way of thinking builds stress, encourages feelings of crisis or emergency, communicates to those around us that our activity is more important than they are, and leaves us feeling incapable of getting things done.

Why is this?

The busy mind responds to whatever need screams the loudest and then develops a false sense of importance. *If I wasn't doing this no one else would. I am the one holding it all together. I am very needed.*

Busyness doesn't come alone, it brings its companions: stress, exhaustion, sleeplessness, worry, fear, and depression, just to name a few. Busyness does not allow time for me, let alone time for others. It does not rest or celebrate accomplishments, because the work is never done. Busyness tells the lies, "Your worth and value come from me. You are nothing and have nothing without me. If you take time for yourself, others will think you are lazy. You will never be a leader if you don't do more than everyone else."

If we are to avoid the trap of Martha, then what should we do? How can we accomplish our goals without being busy?

One day I was attempting to button the loop on my sleeve and could not get the button through the hole. The shirt design provides a nifty way to hold up the rolled sleeve, if the sleeve will actually button.

I tried with my limited left hand and cramped my fingers but became frustrated and had no one to call for help. It then occurred to me that if I turned just so and came at it from a different angle it just might work. After a few tries I achieved my goal. Approaching the situation from a different angle worked. (Of course, it then occurred to me that I could have rolled the sleeves and buttoned them while the shirt was still on the hanger. Yet another angle, but I digress.)

Our goals can be reached without our becoming overwhelmed; we can be achievers. Different people can achieve at different paces and still be successful. We just have to find what angle works for us. We all want to be successful in what God has called us to do. Can we accomplish that without giving in to busyness? Take a moment and write down anyone who comes to mind (either from the Bible or someone you know) that can inspire and encourage you to be an achiever.

An achiever does not have to be the best at what he or she does. Achievers simply do what they know they should be doing. They do what is right, what is pleasing to God, and what they have been gifted to do. Yes, we all have responsibilities that do not play into our giftings, but those can be identified, organized, and categorized to certain times in your schedule so they do not become a source of busyness in your day.

The story of Job gives us a great example of an achiever who did not let busyness control him. Job accumulated enormous wealth, had servants to manage, community responsibilities to fulfill, a family to care for, and many people that came to him for counsel. Yet he was not busy. How do we know this? Because busy people don't have time.

Listen to what Job said concerning his daily life:

> All who heard me praised me. All who saw me spoke well of me. For I assisted the poor in their need and the orphans who required help. I helped those without hope, and they blessed me. And I caused the widows' hearts to sing for joy. Everything I did was honest. Righteousness covered me like a robe, and I wore justice like a turban. I served as eyes for the blind and feet for the lame. I was a father to the poor and assisted strangers who needed help" (Job 29:11–16).

Look at what Job did for his family:

When these celebrations ended—sometimes after several days—Job would purify his children. He would get up early in the morning and offer a burnt offering for each of them. For Job said to himself, "Perhaps my children have sinned and have cursed God in their hearts." This was Job's regular practice (Job 1:5).

Notice what God said about Job:

Then the LORD asked Satan, "Have you noticed my servant Job? He is the finest man in all the earth. He is blameless-- a man of complete integrity. He fears God and stays away from evil" (Job 1:8).

Finally, read Job's response when tragedy struck:

He said, "I came naked from my mother's womb, and I will be naked when I leave. The LORD gave me what I had, and the LORD has taken it away. Praise the name of the LORD!" (Job 1:21)

FOCUS THOUGHT

The first thing a busy life steals is my relationships.

Job could not have been living under the influence of busyness. He was praised for the time he spent helping the poor. Those he helped blessed him and sang because of him. They not only received his help, but they also felt hope and joy, and they had a relationship with him as their father. They did not feel he was too busy for them, they felt valued by him.

Job took time for his family. He knew his children's schedules, even though they were adults. This takes intentionality and consistent communication. Job prayed, sacrificed for them, and purified them before the Lord. He made time for his children and continually exemplified the importance of God's laws.

Job also had a relationship with God and did not reject that relationship when he was hurting. His identity was tied to that relationship and not to his possessions or social status. Job is a great example of an achiever: a person who lived intentionally, without being busy.

Stress, anxiety, exhaustion, and discouragement are the companions of a busy life. Yes, at times life can be crazy, but the companions of busyness do not have to be ours.

Why is this important? Because the first thing a busy lifestyle steals is our relationships and quickly tries to replace them with its own. If we allow the companions of busyness to dictate our lives, we will find less and less time for those we love, while the voice of busyness keeps saying that everything we are doing is for them.

Neither Martha nor Job had control of the unexpected situations they were in (Martha's guests and Job's tragedies), but they had very different responses. Our responses to the unexpected come out of how we are already living our lives, not from the immediate situations.

How can you live as an achiever? List some areas of your life that have been taken over by busyness.

How can you change these areas from being controlled by busyness to becoming areas of achievement?

_____

_____

_____

_____

_____

_____

_____

_____

PRAYER

As you begin to remove the chokehold of busyness in your life, let Psalm 119:32–37 become a prayer that will sustain you. Write it down, place it somewhere you will see every day, and pray it aloud.

I will pursue your commands, for you expand my understanding. Teach me your decrees, O LORD; I will keep them to the end. Give me understanding and I will obey your instructions; I will put them into practice with all my heart. Make me walk along the path of your commands, for that is where my happiness is found. Give me an eagerness for your laws rather than a love for money! Turn my eyes from worthless things, and give me life through your word (Psalm 119:32–37).

PRAISE

How can you infuse praise into your day?

_____

_____

_____

_____

_____

_____

_____

THANKSGIVING

List someone or something you are thankful for today and why.

_____

_____

_____

_____

_____

_____

_____

_____

ASK WITH BELIEF

Ask God for something today. Whether it in involves inspiration, spiritual growth, or resolution of a problem, just remember to believe that He will answer you!

3

DISTRACTION:
THE BACKGROUND NOISE OF LIFE

IN YOUR BIBLE

2 Kings 5:1–27

FOCUS VERSE

I appeal to you, dear brothers and sisters, by the authority of our Lord Jesus Christ, to live in harmony with each other. Let there be no divisions in the church. Rather, be of one mind, united in thought and purpose (1 Corinthians 1:10).

THE PHONE RANG AND, not wanting the kids to hear the conversation, I stepped away for just a moment. Passing the dryer, I remembered the clothes that had been dry since last night and started folding them as I talked. Accomplishing two things at once, I was feeling pretty successful until I smelled dinner going up in smoke.

How could I forget the food on the stove! If this had been the first time, I would have been shocked, but instead I felt disgusted that I had, again, been distracted. *At least it wasn't boiled eggs*, I said to myself. That explosive episode of distraction had cost me a pan, gained me a stinky house, and left me cleaning egg off the ceiling and cabinets. I was finding egg in surprising places a month later.

My series of distractions, while humorous now, could have led to devastation (such as a fire) had they not been discovered. Why does this keep happening to me? Why do distractions seem to overcome my good intentions so often? How does the noise of life get so loud that I forget my good intentions altogether? As I examine these distractions more closely, I realize they are another culprit choking my life.

In 2 Kings 5 the story of Naaman and Gehazi hits home. Naaman has a chance at something unheard of, to be healed of leprosy. He left with the best of intentions, but was distracted from his purpose by pride and anger. Gehazi, the servant to Elisha, was distracted from his purpose by wealth. Could he have been the next great prophet after Elisha? That will remain a mystery because his distractions cost him and his family everything. Many times, distractions lead to temptation, and temptation leads to sin. But what if we can learn to overcome distractions before they get loud enough to capture our attention?

FOCUS THOUGHT

Distraction can overcome good intentions, but it cannot displace a developed purpose.

When we have purpose we have identity, validation, direction, focus, and unity. We must clear away the distractions that choke us to make space for God's clear, unmistakable purpose for our lives.

> They will be my people, and I will be their God. And I will give them one heart and one purpose: to worship me forever, for their own good and for the good of all their descendants (Jeremiah 32:38–39).

> And we know that God causes everything to work together for the good of those who love God and are called according to his purpose for them (Romans 8:28).

Do you know what your purpose is? Have you spent much time thinking about it? If not, don't panic. You are not alone. If you had a purpose but lost sight of it, you are not alone. Even David, the future king of Israel, struggled with keeping sight of God's plan for his life.

I cry out to God Most High, to God who will fulfill his purpose for me (Psalm 57:2).

The following list of verses focuses on God's purpose for all of humanity. Grab your Bible and read through these. Take notes on any that you feel God is specifically using to speak to you now as He continues to fulfill His purpose in you.

Mark 1:15	Acts 1:5
Mark 16:16	Acts 2:38, 41
John 20:31	Acts 10:45–48
Galatians 3:22–28	Acts 16:28–33
I Thessalonians 4:14–18	Acts 19:4–5
I Timothy 1:15–16	Acts 22:16
James 2:19–26	Colossians 2:12
I John 3:23–24	I Corinthians 12:13
Psalm 7:10–12	II Corinthians 1:21–22
Matthew 3:2	Ephesians 1:13
Matthew 3:11	Mark 16:15
Luke 5:32	Matthew 22:37–39
Luke 24:47–49	Luke 6:27–31
Acts 2:37–39	John 13:34–35
Acts 3:19	Colossians 3:11–15
Mark 1:4	

After reading through these verses, what would you say is God's purpose for the believer?

_____

_____

_____

_____

_____

_____

_____

What is God asking you to do for Him? What is your purpose in His kingdom?

_____

_____

_____

_____

_____

_____

_____

If this is the foundation for purpose in your life, how can you use your giftings and abilities to accomplish that purpose?

_____

_____

_____

_____

_____

_____

_____

PRAYER

Take time to pray about the things that distract you. Some things may be glaringly obvious, but God may need to reveal others as you talk with Him and listen for His voice. Make a list of what distracts you from your purpose.

_____

_____

_____

_____

_____

_____

You are valuable to God and a benefit to His kingdom, and He desires to shelter you from the noise that tries to overwhelm you.

The godly will rejoice in the LORD and find shelter in him. And those who do what is right will praise him (Psalm 64:10).

Allow God to help you focus on your purpose, and learn how to prevent and overcome distractions. This is another important step in removing the things that are choking you.

PRAISE

Take a few minutes and list some areas where you are successfully overcoming distractions. Give God praise that He has already given you success in these areas and is already helping you overcome the distractions you listed earlier.

THANKSGIVING

What are you thankful for today?

ASK WITH BELIEF

Do you have a specific distraction that only God can help you overcome? God will work in the situation, He will answer your prayer. Write out what you need in faith and watch Him work.

4

TEMPTATION:
THE PULL TO ABANDON YOUR PURPOSE FOR PLEASURE

IN YOUR BIBLE

James 1:12–16

FOCUS VERSE

Have mercy on me, O God, have mercy! I look to you for protection. I will hide beneath the shadow of your wings until the danger passes by (Psalm 57:1).

HAVE YOU EVER FOUND yourself sitting at a red light at a time of night that most people are in bed and you really want to be in yours? Me too. It seems that light stays red *so long* and there is *no one* on the road but me, so why sit there and waste *my* time obeying a law that should only apply when more than one vehicle is on the road?

These are the thoughts that rapidly make their way out of my mouth as my husband and I wait there, propping open our eyelids. My ever-consistent conscience (my husband), quietly speaks my name as a reminder that I am about to cross a line, no matter my excuses.

Does temptation ever sneak up on you like this, with a million reasons why this rule or protection is not applicable in this situation? What about the suggestion that this is not really a problem for you, it's just a guard for people who do have a problem. The Apostle Paul addressed this very issue in his letter to the Galatian church.

Dear brothers and sisters, if another believer is overcome by some sin, you who are godly should gently and humbly help that person back onto the right path. And be careful not to fall into the same temptation yourself (Galatians 6:1).

If there was no possibility of you falling into that trap, then there would be no need of a warning. One of temptation's most successful lies is, "That does not apply to you."

Have you ever taken a walk through a field or tall grassy area? I have, and it was obviously a beautiful day or I would not have been out walking. I was minding my own business when a stinging pain shot through my leg. My initial thought was I had been bitten. Whatever it was, it commanded all my attention.

Upon close examination, I found not a bite, but a tiny scratch that produced a massive burning sensation. I looked around and there they were! A handful of leaves with tiny needles. A Stinging Nettle. Oh, how I despise these plants!

Whether I wanted to or not, the wound from the Stinging Nettle was all I could think about until the burning subsided (which can take days without quick and proper treatment).

Temptation loves to catch us off guard with such an intensity that we can think of nothing else. The potency with which it attaches itself is overwhelming, and, without the correct treatment, we will give in. It is in the times we least expect that temptation can become the most aggressive. But even then, God will give us a way out.

If you think you are standing strong, be careful not to fall. The temptations in your life are no different from what others experience. And God is faithful. He will not allow the temptation to be more than you can stand. When you are tempted, he will show you a way out so that you can endure (1 Corinthians 10:12–13).

What is the treatment for temptation?

Scripture gives some very direct instruction. Matthew 26:14 and Luke 22:40 teach us to pray specifically concerning temptation. If we are praying against temptation, then we will remain vigilant and harder to catch off guard. Praying for help against temptation encourages humility and is a good reminder that we all need a Savior; not just those who still don't know Him.

1 Timothy 6:6–10 speaks of the importance of contentment, for, without it, we will give into our temptations. Mostly those rooted in the love of money. There are those who attain wealth and those who do not, but both can become lovers of wealth. A love that will eventually destroy them. However, contentment is the antidote to loving wealth, no matter what the income.

The book of James gives us real life instruction for our struggles.

> Confess your sins to each other and pray for each other so that you may be healed. The earnest prayer of a righteous person has great power and produces wonderful results (James 5:16).

What if we took this principle and applied it to temptation? I am in no way encouraging you to share your temptations or sins with everyone. But I once received the very wise counsel to find someone I could trust and be accountable to that person. (This person should not be of the opposite sex unless he/she is your spouse.) This is a very powerful tool in overcoming temptation. When you can't think clearly, you have someone who will help you.

Another very important scriptural tool to combat temptation is found in Matthew 4:1–10, when Jesus was tempted by Satan. He continually responded to Satan's enticements by quoting Scripture. The power of Scripture will never fail!

Plan ahead. Write down some Scriptures, memorize them if you can, and then it will be even harder for the enemy to catch you off guard, because you will be ready with Scripture.

FOCUS THOUGHT

Temptation lures me with promise but leaves me with condemnation!

Temptation tries to convince you that "it doesn't really matter." It tries to catch you off guard and disorient you, while it whispers lies in your ear. Temptation is another force that is trying to choke you. Jesus instructed His disciples to pray against temptation, and He gave us the example of quoting Scripture when faced with temptation. He also encouraged us to help one another and promised to be our Deliverer.

> God is our refuge and strength, always ready to help in times of trouble (Psalm 46:1).

PRAYER

Psalm 18 and Psalm 145 are excellent to pray aloud, choose one or both to use in your time of prayer today.

PRAISE

Write out a praise to God, the One who covers you with His protection, forgives you by His grace, and always makes a way of escape.

THANKSGIVING

Make a list of prayers that God has answered and give Him thanks.

ASK WITH BELIEF

God hears you when you pray, so what do you need?

5

SIN:
IT'S NOT THAT BAD!

IT WAS THE YEAR 2007, two sons had been born into the Lugo home and life had finally settled into a routine. All was well, love flowed freely, and the entire family felt safe and cared for. And then *The Event.* The event that changed the Lugo marriage forever. It was dramatic, traumatic, and painful; and it left one party wondering just how the other party could be so cold, callus, and heartless.

My husband is the antithesis of dramatic. He is practical, pragmatic, and thinks almost everything through to the most minute detail. He put all these characteristics to work when he purchased a baby gate to keep the kids out of the room with the pretty furniture and the family computer. It had a high star rating, lots of informative comments, it could be screwed to the wall and floor, and had a sturdy door. It would be impossible for our little geniuses to conquer.

One night after the boys were in bed, I was relaxing on the regular comfy couch when I heard a thud and saw my strong, stalwart husband fall to the floor screaming.

I was caught completely off guard. I couldn't imagine that someone could actually break their big toe on a baby gate, so I did what any woman married to such a pragmatic husband would do. I laughed.

I laughed so hard I could not get off the couch. I laughed when he got up. I laughed when he showed it to me, insisting it was broken. I laughed when he said, with exasperation, "You are laughing at me!" I laughed while he called his mother (a nurse) and I laughed the next day when we splinted what was a very broken and bruised big toe.

This reaction did not express the love and affection that my husband had expected in such a traumatic situation. It also didn't help that I kept telling him, "It's not that bad, it just can't be broken." The next morning as I (still giggling) wrapped his toe, he just kept staring at me and saying, "It's not that bad, huh?"

Needless to say, this was a sore spot for a while (pun intended). I could not help the giggles every time he told someone the story. I am still snickering as I write this. Eleven years later!

IN YOUR BIBLE

1 Samuel 15:13–22

FOCUS VERSE

Create in me a clean heart, O God. Renew a loyal spirit within me (Psalm 51:10).

In 1 Samuel 15, Saul was responding to Samuel in the same way that I responded to *The Event*. Saul was not necessarily laughing, but he seemed to feel that Samuel was overreacting.

Samuel was not overreacting.

> Then the LORD said to Samuel, 'I am sorry that I ever made Saul king, for he has not been loyal to me and has refused to obey my command.' Samuel was so deeply moved when he heard this that he cried out to the LORD all night (1 Samuel 15:10–11).

Many of the Old Testament prophets leaned towards the dramatic, and it seems that Saul responded to Samuel with that in mind.

It's really not that bad.

The problem was Saul continually applied this thinking to his decisions, and that thinking eventually cost him the kingdom, God's anointing, and his life.

I really enjoy drinking a Coca Cola with my lunch. I know it is unhealthy, but I justify it by eating healthy and believing that the soda helps settle my stomach.

One day I accidently bought a Diet Coke. When I realized it, I vehemently stated, "I'm not putting that junk in my body with all those chemicals!"

It took just a few seconds before I started laughing, realizing the inconsistency. I was perfectly okay with the ingestion of unhealthy chemicals when it came to my desires, but was adamantly against it when it came to other's.

It is so easy to do this with sin. It is easy to condemn the actions of others with the thought, *I would never do that*, while overlooking the actions in our own lives that are just as harmful. We often justify ourselves by saying:

- It really doesn't bother me
- It's not that bad
- I'm doing really good compared to…
- I've done worse
- Someone else does it and they are fine
- I don't feel any conviction about it (neither did Saul)
- The Bible doesn't say it's a sin
- I'm mature enough to handle it

FOCUS THOUGHT

Am I choking on sin while thinking, It's not that bad?

This very thing is warned against in James:

> So get rid of all the filth and evil in your lives, and humbly accept the word God has planted in your hearts, for it has the power to save your souls. But don't just listen to God's word. You must do what it says. Otherwise, you are only fooling yourselves. For if you listen to the word and don't obey, it is like glancing at your face in a mirror. You see yourself, walk away, and forget what you look like (James 1:21–24).

To prevent being choked out by sin, we must continually search ourselves and ask God to illuminate actions, attitudes, and areas we need to change.

PRAYER

Pray this Scripture and commit it to memory:

> Create in me a clean heart, O God. Renew a loyal spirit within me. Do not banish me from your presence, and don't take your Holy Spirit from me. Restore to me the joy of your salvation, and make me willing to obey you (Psalm 51:10–12).

PRAISE

Take a moment to praise God for His unfailing love, patience, and willingness to call us to change. Write a praise to God for how He changed your thinking concerning a distraction, temptation, or sin in your life.

THANKSGIVING

List why you are thankful for God's mercy. Let this verse inspire you.

Praise the LORD! For he has heard my cry for mercy. The LORD is my strength and shield. I trust him with all my heart. He helps me, and my heart is filled with joy. I burst out in songs of thanksgiving (Psalm 28:6–7).

ASK WITH BELIEF

Reflect on the needs you have written down since you started this study and list any that have been answered. Also, include any new needs you have.

CONFLICT:
NAVIGATING DIFFICULT WATERS WITH A WELL-CHARTED MAP

IN YOUR BIBLE

The Book of Esther

FOCUS VERSE:

Who among you fears the LORD and obeys his servant? If you are walking in darkness, without a ray of light, trust in the LORD and rely on your God (Isaiah 50:10).

DO YOU LIKE CONFLICT?

If you answered, "No," then you would be numbered with the majority of humanity. Some people like recreational arguing, verbal bantering, or airing their grievances, but very few people actually like conflict. In fact, some who work in the field of mental health believe people who thrive on conflict may have a personality disorder.

As much as we don't like conflict, it still happens. We must learn how to work through it or it will choke us off from the vital things we need to grow in order to draw closer to God.

The Book of Esther provides excellent examples of how to conduct ourselves in conflict and how to work to bring that conflict to resolution. Every conflict will have its own story, but Esther's story provides the tools needed to successfully navigate most of the conflicts we face. As we study Esther's story, this Scripture must be front and center:

You will keep in perfect peace all who trust in you, all whose thoughts are fixed on you! Trust in the LORD always, for the LORD GOD is the eternal Rock (Isaiah 26:3–4).

No matter where we are in the process of conflict resolution, we must keep our thoughts fixed on Jesus and He will be our Rock, filling us with His peace.

Esther's journey began due to conflict at the palace. Her initial role was to be a part of fixing a problem: look beautiful, smell good, please the king, and, hopefully, qualify as the new queen.

Obviously, smelling nice and smiling should help in any conflict, but let's look a little deeper at what Esther did to help resolve each problem at hand. Esther 2:9–15 reveals that Esther made it a habit to listen to good advice. For instance, she obeyed Mordecai when he instructed her to keep her heritage a secret to prevent more conflict in an already volatile situation.

Later in chapter 2, Esther was again drafted into a conflict when her guardian, Mordecai, informed her of a plot to assassinate the king. Esther made sure this information was delivered to the king and then credited Mordecai with the find. She didn't try to make herself look good, but instead gave credit where it was due.

Key in resolving conflict is communicating correct information and giving credit to whomever deserves it.

We don't see Esther drawn into another conflict for five years, but then it's one for the record books. This was literally a conflict of life and death.

The first thing Esther did was find out the facts (Esther 4:5–9). She then made sure to communicate all the facts (Esther 4:10–12). Finally, Esther continued a practice she had been doing since the start of the narrative, she obeyed the elder in her life.

Notice that she obeyed with wisdom and with a specific plan. She did not act alone, nor did she act without petitioning God (Esther 4:15–17). She spent time in prayer and fasting, and asked others to join her. After she prepared, she did not waiver, but believed like David:

The LORD is my light and my salvation—so why should
I be afraid? The LORD is my fortress, protecting me from
danger, so why should I tremble? (Psalm 27:1).

Esther walked into the king's presence understanding that her God
was with her.

The next part of this story shows Esther's understanding of posture
during conflict (Esther 5:1–8). She humbled herself before the king
and did not point out, in front of the court, that he was drawn into
a scheme that would cost him another queen. If she had brought her
grievances before the royal court, it had the potential to cause the king
extreme embarrassment. She protected the king's reputation above her
own desires and left the impression with the court that she would risk
her own life just to have dinner with the king.

Through our conflicts, we must remember that, like Esther, we are
not alone. God is at work. He does not abandon us to go through conflict alone. Esther 6 is an example of how God works behind the scenes
preparing the hearts of all involved. God is faithful and when we follow
His plan and wait on Him, He will rescue us.

The LORD's light penetrates the human spirit, exposing
every hidden motive (Proverbs 20:27).

He is working on our behalf and knows the intents of the hearts of
those around us and uses that knowledge for His plan and our good.

FOCUS THOUGHT

*Navigating conflict without a plan is like being marooned in a boat with-
out a paddle.*

Esther reminds us in her plea to the king that we should humble
ourselves and speak the truth (Esther 7:3–4). Esther knew all the facts,
and, when she spoke them, the king listened. She had already proved
that she was not seeking self-promotion, and she had no desire to at-
tack or embarrass him.

Esther 8:3 teaches us that we may need more than one discussion to completely resolve a conflict. Patience and perseverance are key to a full resolution.

Lastly, when given someone's trust, understand that responsibility and do not take it lightly (Esther 8:8). Listed below is a recap of how Esther resolved conflict.

1. Listened to and followed good advice

2. Knew the facts

3. Communicated correct and necessary information

4. Gave credit to those who deserved it

5. Listened to and obeyed the leaders in her life

6. Prayed and fasted for guidance (included others when possible)

7. Did not embarrass others

8. Remembered that God was working

9. Had as many discussions as it took to resolve the conflict

10. Treated with care the trust someone gave her

Conflict can make us feel like darkness is closing in and there is no hope, but we must allow Scripture to encourage us.

> You light a lamp for me. The LORD, my God, lights up my darkness (Psalm 18:28).

As we respond to the Lord's call, and clear away the things that are trying to choke us, we must remember we are not in this alone. Esther knew she did not want to face her situation alone, so she asked others to join with her and be a strength along the way. If you are in a place of conflict or struggling through any of these devotions, please find someone you can trust and ask him/her to walk with you. God is with you and He is already working where you cannot see.

PRAYER

Take a few minutes to pray this Scripture. Then pray about this devotion, asking God how it should be applied in your life.

But LORD, be merciful to us, for we have waited for you. Be our strong arm each day and our salvation in times of trouble (Isaiah 33:2).

PRAISE

The Psalms are full of praise for God's deliverance and mighty hand of protection. Do you know a song of praise that communicates how God has rescued you? If so, now is a good time to sing and praise Him!

THANKSGIVING

Give thanks despite a hard situation. Write words of thanksgiving into your circumstance.

_____

_____

_____

_____

_____

_____

_____

_____

ASK WITH BELIEF

List some conflicts in which you would like God to intervene.

7

COMPARING:
THE IDENTITY THIEF

IN YOUR BIBLE

Daniel 1

FOCUS VERSE

Thank you for making me so wonderfully complex! Your workmanship is marvelous—how well I know it (Psalm 139:14).

THE BEGINNING OF Daniel's story finds him in a new place with a new set of circumstances: living as a captive. His home, family, and name had been stripped away, and now he was a nobody in a new land. The goal of the governing power was to bring everyone together and merge them into one people, with one king, and one identity. They would become Babylonian. By changing the captives' location, placing them in a new culture, re-educating them, and giving them new laws to follow, the Babylonians were successfully assimilating entire societies into their own.

We see in Daniel's story the way the Babylonians monitored the captives' assimilation was by comparison. By comparing the captives' diet, language, physical appearance, and knowledge of the laws and customs of the land, the Babylonians could tell which ones were assimilating best. The pressure to conform must have been immense. If the captives were found lacking, what would happen? Would they become slaves—menial servants—or possibly even face death? By using the tool of comparison, the Babylonians were successfully stealing the identity of entire societies.

Take a minute to describe yourself in terms of identity. Who are you?

_____

_____

_____

_____

_____

_____

_____

Did you find it difficult to describe your identity without associating yourself with a location, a people, a culture, your education, or your abilities? How did Daniel and his companions manage to keep their identities intact when all these things were stripped away?

We find the answer to this question in Jeremiah.

But blessed are those who trust in the LORD and have made the LORD their hope and confidence (Jeremiah 17:7).

Where we place our confidence determines our identity.

Have we been misled in our belief that to be fulfilled we must have confidence in ourselves and abilities? There will always be someone smarter, better, lovelier, more favored, and more successful. Our confidence must not originate with our surroundings, self-reliance, abilities, or personal qualities. If it does, what happens when we are relocated, fail, receive negative criticism, or are confronted with our own inadequacies? What happens is an identity crisis.

Somewhere leading into this crisis of identity, *comparisons* happened. Making comparisons is a tool we use in communication and when making decisions. We compare meals, clothes, houses, work, weather, vehicles, and the lists go on. However, when it comes to our identity, we must only compare ourselves with God's ideal, using the mirror of Scripture.

> But don't just listen to God's word. You must do what it says. Otherwise, you are only fooling yourselves. For if you listen to the word and don't obey, it is like glancing at your face in a mirror. You see yourself, walk away, and forget what you look like. But if you look carefully into the perfect law that sets you free, and if you do what it says and don't forget what you heard, then God will bless you for doing it (James 1:22–25).

You and I are set free by the Word of God working in our lives. When we use the mirror of Scripture to find our identity in Christ and when we only compare ourselves to what He wants, it leaves no room for a crisis of identity. God does not, and never will, have an identity crisis.

FOCUS THOUGHT

If I don't know who I am, I won't know where I am going; and I will wind up lost.

Daniel experienced intense change and loss, and was in the perfect situation to have his identity stolen when he was compared to others. Instead of giving in, Daniel 1:8 says, "But Daniel made up his mind." Daniel had already found his identity in the one and only God, and when your identity is found in Him look what happens:

> God gave these four young men an unusual aptitude for understanding every aspect of literature and wisdom. And God gave Daniel the special ability to interpret the meanings of visions and dreams. When the training

period ordered by the king was completed, the chief of staff brought all the young men to King Nebuchadnezzar. The king talked with them, and no one impressed him as much as Daniel, Hananiah, Mishael, and Azariah. So they entered the royal service (Daniel 1:17–19).

Do you sometimes find yourself choking on the fear of what others think and how you measure up, or just wishing you were more like someone else? Let these words from Galatians challenge you.

Pay careful attention to your own work, for then you will get the satisfaction of a job well done, and you won't need to compare yourself to anyone else (Galatians 6:4).

God is calling you to come to Him. He knows where you are broken, but He also knows where you are gifted, and He wants you to find your identity in Him. He can heal the brokenness, and He can exalt your giftings, but only if your identity is not stolen through the trap of comparing yourself to others.

PRAYER

Take a moment and pray this prayer. As you do, list the things that are trying to pull your identity in God away from you.

Search me, O God, and know my heart; test me and know my anxious thoughts. Point out anything in me that offends you, and lead me along the path of everlasting life (Psalm 139:23–24).

PRAISE

Declare this Scripture aloud, personalizing it with "I" and "me," as your praise today.

But you are not like that, for you are a chosen people. You are royal priests, a holy nation, God's very own possession. As a result, you can show others the goodness of God, for he called you out of the darkness into his wonderful light. Once you had no identity as a people; now you are God's people. Once you received no mercy; now you have received God's mercy (1 Peter 2:9–10).

THANKSGIVING

List ways having a relationship with Jesus has given you an identity in Him.

ASK WITH BELIEF

Think about how comparing has affected you, and list specific things you would like God to help you with and bring healing to.

8

FAILURE:
THE ENEMY OF HOPE

IN YOUR BIBLE

Isaiah 51:5–12

FOCUS VERSE

But joyful are those who have the God of Israel as their helper, whose hope is in the LORD their God (Psalm 146:5).

EVERYONE FAILS! No one likes it, and many would prefer not to talk about their failures, but that doesn't change the truth. Failure is unpleasant—no—failure is awful. There is no way to make failure look good, better, or even tolerable, and it is impossible to hide it for very long. On a slightly encouraging note, other than Jesus, can you think of one biblical character who did not fail?

As I read my Bible and take note of the many failures of humanity, I also notice a trend. After a failure, a multitude of both negative and positive opportunities are presented. Some negative opportunities include attempting to hide, allowing frustration or anger to take control, having an attitude of apathy, wallowing in self-pity, blaming God, blaming others, and even experiencing immediate death (especially in the Old Testament).

Conversely, some of the positive opportunities include acknowledging the failure, repenting of the offense, seeking restoration, asking for help, learning and growing from failure, and believing God is a healer and deliverer who still has a future for you. The voice of our enemy, the devil, will try to use your failure to frustrate you into responding negatively. This voice will tell you that everyone is talking about you, no one believes in you, and you have no hope of future success. Our accuser would like to convince you to give up. And while he is whispering convincing lies in your ear, condemnation will slowly put you in a choke hold. But wait! God knows we fail, and He has a plan.

So humble yourselves under the mighty power of God, and at the right time he will lift you up in honor. Give all your worries and cares to God, for he cares about you. Stay alert! Watch out for your great enemy, the devil. He prowls around like a roaring lion, looking for someone to devour. Stand firm against him, and be strong in your faith. Remember that your Christian brothers and sisters all over the world are going through the same kind of suffering you are (1 Peter 5:6–9).

Failure is so awful because it usually leaves someone hurt, and seriously exposes and wounds our pride. Unfortunately, when it comes to pride, I think I have a double dose. Many times, I catch myself trying to do something better, not because of my desire to do a job well, but because of what others might think. I worry and fret because if I fail, I might lose the confidence of those who trust me. I don't want to disappoint, make others unhappy, or fall short in their eyes. I want to be *amazing*, I want to help others achieve their dreams and possibly be a super hero. This may sound silly, but, alas, it is the truth.

The problem with these statements is the focus: I. When I am the focus, my failure will be magnified and then I am devastated. This is the perfect opportunity for the deceiver to come whisper in my ear and allow my failure to choke me. On the other hand, if I can humble myself and place my focus on Jesus, then I have a helper.

But joyful are those who have the God of Israel as their helper, whose hope is in the LORD their God (Psalm 146:5).

If God is my Help, my Hero, and my Rescuer, and His Word is my guide, then I have hope. I have hope because when I fail, my trust is in God's Word, which never fails. My trust was never in me to start with.

> You are my refuge and my shield; your word is my source of hope (Psalm 119:114).

When my hope is in Jesus (instead of myself) and I fail, then my hope is not crushed. Who I am is found in Him, and no matter what others think, say, or do, I am His and He is my Encourager.

> When doubts filled my mind, your comfort gave me renewed hope and cheer (Psalm 94:19).

Let's reflect on Isaiah 51:5–12. God was speaking to His people who were in captivity and had turned their hearts back to Him. He encouraged them, reminding them that He had the power to rescue and restore them. He also encouraged them not to worry about what others said, because their hope was in Him. He was their Comforter and Deliverer.

The same God speaks to us today. Will you allow Him to be the focus of your life, your decisions, and your desires? Will you give Him your failure and allow Him to bring hope back into your situation? Listening to His voice requires humility, honesty, and the loss of full control, but what is that when He is offering comfort, peace, and a hope that endures for all eternity?

FOCUS THOUGHT

I cannot live failure free, but I can live free of failure.

Do you have failure that you have been struggling with? Has it become a weight you hope others don't notice? Or is it obvious to others, but you don't want to address it? Take a few minutes to write out your thoughts concerning your own failures and what you can do to overcome the chokehold failure wants to put you in.

PRAYER

Let this be your prayer today, pray it aloud to encourage yourself in the Lord.

A psalm of David. I give you thanks, O LORD, with all my heart; I will sing your praises before the gods. I bow before your holy Temple as I worship. I praise your name for your unfailing love and faithfulness; for your promises are backed by all the honor of your name. As soon as I pray, you answer me; you encourage me by giving me strength. Every king in all the earth will thank you, LORD, for all of them will hear your words. Yes, they will sing about the LORD's ways, for the glory of the LORD is very great. Though the LORD is great, he cares for the humble, but he keeps his distance from the proud. Though I am surrounded by troubles, you will protect me from the anger of my enemies. You reach out your hand, and the power of your right hand saves me. The LORD will work out his plans for my life—for your faithful love, O LORD, endures forever. Don't abandon me, for you made me (Psalm 138:1-8).

PRAISE

List some things that you can praise God for during a time of failure.

THANKSGIVING

Look back at a past failure and list some good things that came out of that situation.

_____

_____

_____

_____

_____

_____

_____

ASK WITH BELIEF

In regard to failure, what are some things you need God to do for you and work in you?

_____

_____

_____

_____

_____

_____

_____

Finally, remember:

Hope deferred makes the heart sick, but a dream fulfilled is a tree of life (Proverbs 13:12).

Place your hopes and dreams in Jesus Christ, the One who does all things well.

9

LOSS:
SIN'S FIRST GIFT

IN YOUR BIBLE

Ruth 1

FOCUS VERSES

Let all that I am wait quietly before God, for my hope is in him. He alone is my rock and my salvation, my fortress where I will not be shaken. My victory and honor come from God alone. He is my refuge, a rock where no enemy can reach me. O my people, trust in him at all times. Pour out your heart to him, for God is our refuge (Psalm 62:5–8).

AS YOU READ RUTH chapter one, it is clear Naomi has suffered great loss. She was greatly loved by her daughters-in-law but consumed with the loss of her husband and sons. She returned home empty, blaming God for her suffering and readily acknowledging she was bitter. She had no desire to catch up with old friends, rejoice for the new wealth of crops, or have any ties to the woman she was.

What is fascinating about this story is that Scripture does not condemn Naomi. Instead of condemning her, God provided a way of restoration for her through her daughter-in-law Ruth. While she was bitter towards God, He was working out a plan that would bring her joy and restore life to her family lineage. What started out as a story filled with pain and loss, ended with a message of hope to all who walk the same road.

Due to many types of loss, we can end up confused, disoriented, angry, depressed, and even bitter. Have you experienced loss, expected or unexpected, that has left you feeling like this? Can you write about it?

_____

_____

_____

_____

_____

_____

_____

_____

_____

While reading through the Old Testament, I commented to my husband, "This is so hard. Reading about the failure of humanity and the judgment of God is hard to get through. I feel so heavy."

The Lord spoke to me and said, "I have experienced loss too."

I then realized that God understood Naomi's feelings. He has experienced rejection, been lied to, seen His children destroy themselves and others, been laughed at, mocked, used, criticized, blamed, ignored, misrepresented, and much more. All before the stories of the New Testament ever took place!

As I read in Jerimiah about the fierce judgement coming upon Israel, the land, and the expression of God's anger; I saw a theme continuing throughout the book. God continually asked His people to repent and turn back to Him, so He could turn away the judgement and their future would be different. At the same time judgement was prophesied, God continually offered a way of escape for His people, hoping they would choose the path of restoration.

God did the same thing in Naomi's story. While she was hurt and bitter, He planned for her healing and restoration. He worked in the hearts of Ruth and Boaz to bring this plan to pass. Ruth experienced loss as well, and God helped her through her own pain to bring comfort to Naomi. Because Ruth suffered as Naomi had, Naomi accepted comfort from Ruth when she rejected it from the other ladies in the community. Paul references this same pattern of comforting others in 2 Corinthians.

> He comforts us in all our troubles so that we can comfort others. When they are troubled, we will be able to give them the same comfort God has given us (2 Corinthians 1:4).

God not only walks with us during times of loss by giving us encouragement through His Word and Spirit, He also puts other people in our lives to help us. Who are the people in your life you can turn to for comfort when you are hurting?

_____

_____

_____

_____

_____

_____

Loss overwhelmed Naomi and her hope was slowly choked out, but God did not give up on her. He continued to call her, and when she realized that He was working out a plan, her hope sparked back to life. She then became involved in her own healing and restoration. What a great gift hope is! You can be blinded by the darkness of loss and feel like you are living in a tomb of despair with only God's strength giving you breath. Then, in a moment, with one spark of hope the darkness is pushed back and a new future is illuminated. God takes your hand and says, "This is what I have been working on for you."

If you have lost hope, feel condemnation, and think that you are already choked lifeless, don't give up. No, our God is working, planning, creating and preparing a new future for you. One full of hope, joy, and strength.

I had a true friend who experienced much loss. She lost her father at a young age (because he chose to leave her mother), her self-esteem because of the unkindness of others, her self-respect when she believed a lie, a career advancement due to another's jealousy, her freedom due to abuse, and eventually she lost herself to fear. Her life sounds like a tragedy, and it was, until one day, through unique circumstances, she met Jesus. When she did, oh, what a day! She had never felt so loved and wanted. She had come face to face with her True Love. One that would never reject her and who filled her with a joy she had not known could exist.

Close to thirty years later, weeks away from retirement, she sat in a doctor's office and listened as he explained her type of cancer was extremely rare and very aggressive with no treatment options. She asked God for a healing, but He replied that it was time for her to come home. She looked at her family, understanding what it meant to suffer great loss, and made a decision based on hope.

She spoke to me about her life before Christ and after. She discussed her suffering, mistakes, regrets, frustrations, and joys. She laughed, cried, and then said, "I have taught my children how to live for God. How to live right. Now I am going to teach them how to die right.'"

I was stunned! She looked death in the face and praised God. She sang, worshipped, and honored the One who had never left her side, who gave her peace in the storms, and encouragement during very dark days. She understood that loss could be a force that chokes out life and relationship with God, and she wanted none of her children to be robbed of their first love due to loss.

I watched her pass from this life with the presence of God filling the room. Her children who were present experienced His power in a way that is hard to put into words. Death was truly swallowed up in victory! (See 1 Corinthians 15:54.) Her exit from this life left no doubt in the minds of all present that we most assuredly have a future hope, and that Christ is returning for His people. She gave this gift to her children because she refused to allow loss to take control and choke her. She knew her life could not be lost, since she had already given it to her true love and Savior, Jesus Christ.

FOCUS THOUGHT

Hope is the spark that starts the flame that lights the path to my future.

PRAYER

Take time to pray these Scriptures today and let them strengthen you and begin to birth hope into your loss: Psalm 9:9, Psalm 61:1-4, Psalm 33:20-22, Psalm 94:17-19. Write out one that speaks to you today, or one that you would like to memorize.

PRAISE

As soon as I pray, you answer me; you encourage me by giving me strength (Psalm 138:3).

What a praise! God does not promise to give us all the answers, but He does promise strength. Encourage yourself by writing about a time God gave you strength and why you know He will do it again.

THANKSGIVING

During times of loss it can be very difficult to be thankful. Looking back to a previous experience, can you list some things you can give thanks for that happened during that experience? Also, can you write an encouraging thought to yourself that will help you find thankfulness during a time of future loss?

ASK WITH BELIEF

There is so much to pray for during times of loss, and many times there are no words. Born out of your own experience, take a moment to pray for someone else who is suffering loss. Write out your prayer for them and if the time comes when you have no words for yourself, come back to this and pray it for yourself.

10

PAIN:
THE PATH TO A PROVEN LOVE

IN YOUR BIBLE
Colossians 3:12–15

FOCUS VERSE

Is there any encouragement from belonging to Christ? Any comfort from his love? Any fellowship together in the Spirit? Are your hearts tender and compassionate? (Philippians 2:1)

WHEN I EXPERIENCE something unpleasant, from that point on, I naturally try to avoid whatever caused the unpleasantness. If I burn my hand reaching in the oven, I buy oven mitts. If a waitress drops the drinks she is carrying down my back and then proceeds to yell at me— This has happened to my husband at three different restaurants. Again one of those times I am not supposed to laugh. I failed!—I am not going to want to go back to that restaurant. If someone says something hurtful to me, mocks me, or is extremely rude, then I will begin avoiding them. I can also begin to avoid others who *seem* like they may act in the same manner as someone else who has hurt me. The term I use for this reaction is "building walls." Everyone does it because we are self-preserving beings.

There seems to be no limit to the sources of pain in our world. When an abuse, sickness, or crime is directly addressed, multiple others rise up to take its place. Sin leads to pain, hurt people tend to hurt people, and pain does not stay outside the doors of the church. It comes right in, travelling in the hearts of the hurting (which are all of us).

As God plants His Word in our hearts and we respond, He begins the healing process for the pain we have endured. Some pain is healed instantly as He washes us of our sin and fills us with His Spirit. Other types of pain require more time, wise counsel, and a slower process as God brings healing and restoration.

God is calling you and me to come closer to Him and we are responding. As we do, He shows us things that are trying to choke our relationship with Him. Consistently, we have been studying God's Word, spending time in prayer, and with the help of His Spirit, removing these destructive things that try to choke us.

This lesson addresses one of the deadliest weapons the enemy uses to choke the life of a believer: pain. Not pain inflicted from the sources we expect (due to sin and a broken world), but pain from inside the walls of our safe place, where we have found our new life in the body of Christ: the Church.

Did you ever hear Hans Christian Anderson's story "The Princess and the Pea"?

A prince is searching for a true princess but is unsuccessful. Then, one stormy night, a young lady arrives at the castle gate soaking wet, claiming to be a princess and asking for shelter. Inviting her in for the night, the queen mother is unconvinced she is a real princess and hides a pea under a stack of forty mattresses. The next morning when the young lady is asked how she slept, she responds that her night was terrible. She complains that she slept on something hard and is bruised all over. This proves to the royal family that she was indeed a real princess, for no one else could be so delicate. The prince then makes plans to marry his newly found princess.

When we meet Jesus and are born into His kingdom, we become a part of His family (in essence we are brought out of the storm and rain like the girl in the story). We experience His Spirit, the washing away of our sins, and the newness of walking with Him. We are now in a place where we belong, covered by God's blood and made a part of

His family. As God pours His love into us, it begins to shine out from around the walls and rough places we have built inside.

When God pours His love into us, something begins to happen. As His love flows through us, it pushes through the walls we have built. It begins to heal us, and the walls start falling, some more quickly than others. We begin to feel different, lighter, and new. The rough places are smoothed, and God's gentle love begins to sooth our spirit as we feel a sensitivity to Him and others. We feel love for others and our new family has become a place of laughter, love, and refuge. Scripture comes alive and we feel the love that has covered our multitude of sins.

Most important of all, continue to show deep love for each other, for love covers a multitude of sins (1 Peter 4:8).

Thankfulness fills our hearts and we begin to forgive others as we realize that so many people don't know Jesus. It gets easier to love others because we are sensitive to their pain and we can finally see past ourselves to their need. We might make comments such as, "Living for God is amazing!" "A life with God's presence is so full of peace and joy." And "I didn't know life could be like this."

Then one day the unthinkable happens; someone in your new family does something that hurts you. The pain is shocking, and you are completely unprepared to be hurt by someone in the Church. What do you do? How should you respond? How could they do this and call themselves a child of God?

If this ugliness had happened before Jesus, it could have been blown off, bouncing off your well-constructed walls. That is, if your walls would have even allowed you to be in a position for it to happen at all. But now you are living a life exposed by God's love. You are sensitive and you care.

The automatic reaction to this pain is to reconstruct your walls, quickly for your own protection. While those walls keep others out, they also keep God's love in. His love is meant to be given, shared, and poured out; so, confusion sets in. *If I continue to be sensitive, I am going to experience pain. If I rebuild my walls, I will feel protected. But they will inhibit God's love from flowing through me! If I want to keep my*

LORD I AM COMING

walls and have God's love, then I will need to allow only a trickle of His love into my spirit. If I allow God's love to completely fill me, then it will begin to break down my walls and I might get hurt again.

What a conundrum!

Read Colossians 3:12–15 again. This passage does not tell us to hide sin or allow abuse in the church, but it does remind us that we are going to get on each other's nerves, and even hurt each other at times. We are made sensitive through God's love; we empathize with others, hurt and laugh with them, see when someone is in need, and reach out to them in love. To be that open and sensitive means that things are going to hurt us. The princess in our story was bruised while inside the palace. She was hurt inside the place she sought refuge; the place where she belonged. Even in a place as safe and loving as the Church, there are times we will end up bruised.

Jesus did not give us this great sensitivity and then abandon us to be hurt by anyone and everyone. He continually pours His love on us and will bring us through our pain to a place of true forgiveness and healing. Then He will show us how we have grown; we have learned to forgive, trust, and love someone else better than ourselves. He will let us experience the joy of helping someone else through their pain.

Conversely, when times of pain come, our enemy is waiting to plant seeds of his own and then allow your pain to fertilize them. Seeds of anger, resentment, sadness, cynicism, and bitterness can grow into our lives and begin to choke out our relationship with God. These seeds cause us to distrust others, isolate ourselves, blame those around us and even God for our pain. To protect us from this wicked plan, God instructs us not to seek justice for ourselves, but rather to extend forgiveness.

> Get rid of all bitterness, rage, anger, harsh words, and slander, as well as all types of evil behavior. Instead, be kind to each other, tenderhearted, forgiving one another, just as God through Christ has forgiven you" (Ephesians 4:31–32).

There will be moments when you are bruised by a "hard little pea" and shocked by how something so small can hurt so much. Then, there will be situations when you feel like you were told to climb onto forty mattresses to sleep (and did so in obedience), and then were pushed off. In the midst of the pain, you hear, "What kind of idiot climbs onto forty mattresses?" It also sounds like, "What kind of idiot obeys a God they cannot see and lets people close enough to inflict that kind of pain? What kind of love puts others first, risks itself, and then willingly forgives?"

> Dear friends, let us continue to love one another, for love comes from God. Anyone who loves is a child of God and knows God. But anyone who does not love does not know God, for God is love. God showed how much he loved us by sending his one and only Son into the world so that we might have eternal life through him. This is real love-- not that we loved God, but that he loved us and sent his Son as a sacrifice to take away our sins. Dear friends, since God loved us that much, we surely ought to love each other. No one has ever seen God. But if we love each other, God lives in us, and his love is brought to full expression in us (1 John 4:7–12).

FOCUS THOUGHT

True love is only proved through pain and forgiveness.

Everyone experiences pain, and unfortunately, it occurs in the Church as well. Jesus knew this would happen, and left us instructions on how to respond, not only for our own good, but also as a testimony to all around us.

> Your love for one another will prove to the world that you are my disciples (John 13:35).

How can it be proven that you really are a child of the King? What says to all those around you that you really are an heir with Christ? It is your response when you are hurt by those *in* the body of Christ. True love is only proved through pain and forgiveness. What will the world see when you are made sensitive by the love of God, and then hurt?

The answers to the questions in our Focus Verse are found in the next two verses.

> Then make me truly happy by agreeing wholeheartedly with each other, loving one another, and working together with one mind and purpose. Don't be selfish; don't try to impress others. Be humble, thinking of others as better than yourselves (Philippians 2:2–3).

What do you think about these verses in relation to being hurt in the Church?

_____

_____

_____

_____

_____

_____

_____

_____

Have you been hurt or offended by someone in the Church? What was your process to forgive and show love in that situation?

_____

_____

_____

_____

_____

_____

_____

Are you hurting now from a painful situation? If so, can you develop a plan for healing? List things you can do to initiate forgiveness, and someone you can talk to that will give wise counsel and not promote gossip. Write down some positives you would like to see.

_____

_____

_____

_____

_____

_____

_____

_____

PRAYER

Read Romans chapter 12. Write a very specific prayer of forgiveness. No matter what the situation, prayer always makes a difference. At the end of your prayer, add some ways you would like God to bless those that have hurt you (without hoping Romans 12:20 literally happens to them).

PRAISE

List ways you can praise God when you are hurting.

Now take time to do it!

THANKSGIVING

In times of pain it can be hard to feel thankful. What are some things God has done for you in the past that can encourage you in the present?

ASK WITH BELIEF

It's time to ask for help. God never asked us to live for Him alone, or to forgive by our own might, because we cannot. Present your needs to God and then present the needs of others. Thinking outside of ourselves promotes healing.

ENERGIZE:
FINDING WHAT YOU DO WELL

IN YOUR BIBLE

1 Corinthians 12:12–25, Romans 12:6–13

FOCUS VERSE

The human body has many parts, but the many parts make up one whole body. So, it is with the body of Christ (1 Corinthians 12:12).

IF YOU HAD TO choose three food or drink items that you must eat or drink every day, what would they be? Take your time and think about it. You can eat or drink anything else you want, but these three must be eaten every day, without fail.

1. _____

2. _____

3. _____

How did you do? I immediately thought, *Chocolate and Coca-Cola!* After more reflection, I realized there are days when I don't really want chocolate (rarely), my strong love of Coca-Cola is embarrassingly unhealthy, and those are only two things. If I can daily alter my menu as long as three things never change, what do I choose that never goes away?

I asked myself the questions, "What do I eat daily?" "What is my 'go to' food no matter how I feel?" For me, it's tea, toast, and pineapple. These three make me feel energized, calm, and they settle well in my stomach.

If the question had been, "Pick three things and they are the only things you can eat," then my list would be the tea, toast, and pinapple. This question isn't about survival, but consistency and endurance. I can consistently eat these three items happily, I have done so for quite some time, and still greatly enjoy them. These are items that I never had to adapt my taste buds to, nor did someone have to convince me to try them. It was automatic acceptance and sensory unity that made me very content. There are things in life that happen like this. Things we do that come naturally and just seem to be built into our DNA. Solomon addressed this in the following verse of scripture.

> Whatever you do, do well. For when you go to the grave, there will be no work or planning or knowledge or wisdom (Ecclesiastes 9:10).

Notice the phrase, "Whatever you do, do well." My next question is, "What do you do?" Not, "What do you want to do, what do you plan to do, or what does someone else want you to do," but "What do you do?" What comes naturally?

Are you a fixer, organizer, singer, painter, encourager, conqueror, laugher, crafter, etc.? What do you do with ease, without having to give yourself a pep talk or feel guilted into doing? Solomon said to do those things with all your might; do them well. Why? Because when you are dead, you can't!

I read that and thought, *Well, Duh!* Why would someone so wise point out something so very obvious? Everyone knows when you are dead you can't do anything at all, what is Solomon's point? With some reflection an answer began to emerge. Could it be that I get so caught up in the pressures of living my life always striving to do more, filling in gaps, worrying about what others think, comparing myself and trying to be what someone else expects, that I forget the things I am good at and enjoy doing?

We are continually bombarded with new items to try (items that will supposedly make life easier), meetings we need to attend, articles that need to be read if we want to be informed, and social media telling us that if we had it together like everyone else, we would be much happier. We can quickly become overwhelmed, feeling worthless, insignificant, and depressed. It can seem that others are doing so much for God, their families, and their careers, while we are just trying to keep our heads above water. In a world with so many advancements and opportunities for connectivity, why does the feeling of meaninglessness creep into our hearts?

Solomon struggled with this very thing. He was cutting edge for his time and nothing was withheld from him. He tried to experience every option, fulfill every dream, and satisfy every desire, yet it failed to fulfill him. We live in a world trying to do the same. Not only are we following in Solomon's footsteps, but we are also coming to the same overwhelming conclusion he did.

"Everything is meaningless," says the Teacher, "completely meaningless!" (Ecclesiastes 1:2)

When God created you, He did not give you a list of options allowing you to choose how you would be designed. He gave you very specific things you do well, and these are your gifts. You are not limited to these gifts, but these are the things you do naturally, and they energize you. You may have many, or just one or two, but God knew that yours would fit you perfectly, and your gifts are needed in the body of Christ. Solomon spoke of having fun and living the life you have been given, but he encouraged us to focus in on the things we do and do them well. He lost sight of this and warned others against doing the same.

Two examples from Scripture who excelled by focusing on their giftings are the Proverbs 31 woman and the Apostle Paul; both very intimidating figures.

It seems that the Proverbs 31 woman does it all. but, really, she doesn't. (See Proverbs 31:15.) Yes, she is admired, successful, has a plan, and seems to only have good days; but this is an example of excellence, no bad days allowed. I used to think that her worst day would rank higher than my best, and felt so humiliated when I read this chapter, knowing I would never measure up. Then I had a really good day when I noticed a small misconception in my perception of this lady. She had help! *Hello!* She had servants to work with her to accomplish the goals she set. She was energized by what she did well.

The Apostle Paul was highly educated, never seemed to tire, traveled, taught, wrote, discipled, and continually planned to do more. How are we to look at his example and not compare ourselves? How do we not exhaust ourselves for Christ and take on as much as we can possibly bear? Again, the only one who can respond to every need is God. Read closely and you will notice that Paul had help too! He had people who travelled with him, helped him write, teach, work, and disciple others. Where do you read in Scripture that Paul came to someone alone? You don't. Paul did what he could do well and had others to help with what he could not. He was energized by his work and focused on that.

FOCUS THOUGHT

What drains me may energize someone else, so I must let them do it. Now that I am answering God's call to come closer and have a plan to keep back the things that want to choke me, I can breathe! My energy is returning and I can think clearly.

Take a few minutes and write down some things you do (things that come naturally and energize you). Everything matters, nothing is too small or great. If you have trouble, ask a friend to help you.

Now, write out how you can daily use these gifts in the kingdom of God. Let them be your "tea, toast, and pineapple." You will add and subtract other things as you go through seasons of life, but don't get distracted from the things you do well.

_____

_____

_____

_____

_____

_____

_____

Now that you have written down the exciting things, take a minute and list what drains you. Some of these tasks must be done, but limit them. Remember what drains you energizes someone else, so let them do it.

_____

_____

_____

_____

_____

_____

_____

_____

PRAISE

Thank you for making me so wonderfully complex! Your workmanship is marvelous—how well I know it (Psalm 139:14).

Take time to praise God for making you and for the gifts He has given you. You are His creation and of immeasurable value. Many times we point out our faults and focus on our negatives, but start a new habit of praising God for your strengths and the value that He places on you. Write your own psalm of praise.

_____

_____

_____

_____

_____

_____

_____

_____

THANKSGIVING

List things about yourself that you are thankful for. Don't leave this section without writing something, you are important and being thankful for you is important too.

_____

_____

_____

_____

_____

_____

_____

ASK WITH BELIEF

Pray for yourself. Ask God to help you love yourself; not in arrogance, but in true appreciation for how He made you.

A second is equally important: 'Love your neighbor as yourself" (Matthew 22:39).

How can you love your neighbor as yourself if you don't love your-self? Write out your prayer.

HIJACK:
DON'T TURN YOUR HOPE
INTO HEARTACHE

IN YOUR BIBLE

Genesis 15:1–6; 16:1–16; 21:1–10

FOCUS VERSE

Who gives intuition to the heart and instinct to the mind? (Job 38:36)

FINISHING THE PREVIOUS lesson and recognizing that God has gifted you to work in His body should infuse hope and excitement into your day. Not only can you now breathe, you can develop and grow in these abilities that you enjoy. God is not expecting you to exhaust yourself trying to be the member of the body you weren't meant to be!

Once the voices that have been trying to choke you have been silenced, you can better hear the voice of Jesus speaking. As He speaks, there is one more trap to avoid, and, while it might not choke you, it can definitely distract and exhaust you.

God calls, and I come and listen. I daily clear away the things that would choke out our relationship and I am living in hope. God gives me direction and speaks about His plans and desires for my life. I feel excitement, hope for the future and then, it happens. I spend hours giving Him advice on the best way to do it. I create different scenarios in my mind of the possible "what if's," and how I will respond to them.

I have good scenarios and bad, happy endings and sad, and ideas about what people will think, say, and do. It goes on and on; all from God giving me a glimpse into His plans.

God is faithful to remind me that I cannot do my job well if I am using my time trying to do God's job for Him or telling Him how best it should be done. God's rebuke of Job comes to my mind:

"Where were you when I laid the foundations of the earth? Tell me, if you know so much" (Job 38:4).

Ouch! Has God given you promises that you struggle to let Him fulfill in His own timing and plan? What are they?

I am reminded of Sarah, after Abraham was promised a son. Both believed the promise, but Sarah did not trust that God had a plan she could not see. She eventually decided He needed her help and Abraham agreed. After many years of marriage with no children, what brought them to the decision of having another woman bear their child? Was this the first time they had this discussion? Where did this urgency come from and why now? It would seem that sometime after they received the promise from God, Sarah felt compelled to help the process along.

When I start trying to do God's job, I can be very convincing (to myself and those around me) that I have found a logical solution for bringing about God's plan. I can make a case for my cause and since it is a Kingdom cause, it can be easy to get others to come alongside and help make "God's plan" happen. However, God's promise or direction is not a problem He has asked me to solve. He has asked me to do my job and has given me a glimpse into His plans. Not because He needs help, but because He is offering hope for what is to come.

FOCUS THOUGHT

I cannot do my job well if I am using my time trying to do God's job for Him.

In my excitement for the promise He has given, I can fall into the trap of trying to hijack God's plan and make it my own. In doing so, I usually end up with some form of disappointment or confusion concerning God's process, because it didn't happen the way I had envisioned. Not only can I get hurt, but so can others I have involved in my plan; just as Sarah's plan left multiple people hurting. When God fulfills the plan, it is better than I could have ever imagined, with twists, turns, and miracles. I can get so tired from the weight of carrying my own plans for His promises, that I miss out on the joy that comes from the hope He gives during the journey.

How I continually fall into this trap puzzles me, but the Scripture reminds me again, "Whatever you do, do well" (Ecclesiastes 9:10a). I pray that my energy will be used on what I can do, and not on what I want to make God do. This prayer from the Psalms is my constant companion:

> May the words of my mouth and the meditation of my heart be pleasing to you, O LORD, my rock and my redeemer (Psalm 19:14).

PRAYER

Pray through the Lord's Prayer in Matthew 6:9–13. As you read each verse, stop and pray for the things it speaks to in each area of your life. This outline for prayer is a great way to bring focus to your prayer time.

PRAISE

Write a praise of celebration for what God has done during your journey of response to Him.

_____

_____

_____

_____

_____

_____

_____

THANKSGIVING

Write out a testimony that you can share with others. Anytime God does a work in us, He connects us to people who are walking a similar path and need encouragement. Be prepared to share.

ASK WITH BELIEF

Ask God to put others on your mind that you can encourage and share your testimony with as they hear His call to come closer. List them.

CONCLUSION

RUNNING THROUGH the dark, out of breath and panting; fear twists and turns my insides, refusing to allow me to stop and rest. I can feel the press of my accuser as he continues to pursue me with words of condemnation, reminders of past failures, and a barrage of guilt.

I cannot turn to either side, for there awaits the traps of temptation that have been so carefully laid for me. I am exhausted, yet I run. I am choked by the thought of being caught, trapped, and destroyed by my enemy; so my feet continue to move, and exhaustion is my new normal.

I must do more to fight back, to prove that I am worth rescuing, then maybe my Savior will come.

I trip and stumble, the ground comes up to meet me. The impact steals what little breath I have left. I lay stunned, eyes shut, fear consuming me as I gasp for air. Pain racks my legs and I cannot stand. I am wounded and alone in the dark, surrounded by the taunts of my enemy. Over and over I can hear him taunting me with my past, my sins, my failures. My utter uselessness.

I hear that voice again, "The King tried to help you, but you are so easily distracted and manipulated. Look at all He did for you, and the disappointment you turned out to be. Just a little stroking of your pride, some changes to your schedule, and a few offenses mixed in and you are completely off track. Not to mention the temptations you continually give in to. You are not worth rescuing, so why even try?"

My mind is racing, trying to find a way to save myself, but at hearing these words everything slows and I am taken back to another time, a place of desperation where these same words were spoken to me.

"You are not worth rescuing, so why even try?"

I believed these words before I met my Savior. When He came and carried me in His arms to a new life, He gave me purpose and a new name. I thought it was too good to be true. I couldn't understand why He cared for me when I was worth nothing.

Why?

Words begin hammering through my mind. *Why did He save me knowing my weaknesses? Why did He help me and give me an identity in Him if He knew I would fail? Why did I allow myself to be tricked? Why didn't I listen to His warnings? Why did I try to be something He didn't ask of me? Why did I hold on to hurts? Why did I start running and why didn't I run to Him?*

As the many questions fill my mind, I remember that even though I may not understand every "why," I have met "The Answer."

My enemy surrounds me, and the air is thick with his words; but he oversteps and reminds me of too much. I remember the darkness that once dominated my life and I remember that I had no hope of deliverance. I questioned why I was even alive, but I also remember meeting "The Answer."

I know He cannot be far away and is probably just outside my line of vision waiting for me. I turn my head to look into the face of my accuser and whisper, "Jesus, help me."

Everything stills. There is a deathly silence, and I wait. Too tired to lift my head and too broken to feel victory, I lay still and continue to wait. I am not the only one waiting. My enemy holds his breath, hoping that I will be ignored and his opportunity to mock and celebrate can be realized.

I feel the difference before I can see any change. A continuous, rhythmic vibration fills my head as I lay on the ground in darkness. I hear the sharp intake of breath as my enemy feels it as well. His presence begins backing away as a light pierces the darkness surrounding us both. The sound of pounding hooves draws closer and finally stops near my head as the blinding light illuminates the entire area. I sigh in relief as my head is lifted, and then my entire body. He is here: my Savior, my Answer, my King.

He isn't beautiful, his hands are calloused from hours of work, and his muscles are taunt from much lifting and carrying of heavy loads. His face is lined from the many emotions that passed over it and his clothes are designed sturdy for travel. When my eyes finally meet His, the depth of emotion, concern, love, and forgiveness leaves me speechless.

As tears fill my eyes, he grabbs the reigns and says, "Hold on tight to me, we're going home."

Wherever you find yourself in your walk with God, there will never be a time when you cannot respond to Him. He wants you to come to Him. Although He is a King and does not exist to meet your expectations, He is always near, patiently awaiting your response to His voice in your life.

I pray the journey you take is filled with the peace, strength, and joy that only Jesus, our King and Savior, can bring. I pray you walk in the fulness of knowing and responding to Him. I also pray that if you find yourself in a place distant from Jesus and find yourself being choked by the enemy, you will remember His voice. You will remember His delivering power and call out His name. He will come!

The LORD says, "I will rescue those who love me. I will protect those who trust in my name" (Psalm 91:14).

www.ingramcontent.com/pod-product-compliance
Lightning Source LLC
Chambersburg PA
CBHW071236090426
42736CB00014B/3102